Before You Say I Do

A Biblical Perspective

DAMEYAN O. COLE

Before You Say I Do

ISBN-13: 978-1539054191
ISBN-10: 1539054195

Printed in the United States of America.
First Edition published 2016.

DEDICATION

I dedicate this book to my beautiful and
inspiring wife (Patrine) who has helped to make this
dream a reality.

.

CONTENTS

ACKNOWLEDGMENTS

I would like to thank my wife and mom (Valrie Cole), for their invaluable contribution to the editing of this book.

INTRODUCTION

Does God have a blueprint for marriage or are we supposed to figure it out on our own? Are we to choose our own mate or should God be included in our decision making? What is the purpose of marriage and when are we ready for marriage? Are there principles in God's word regarding marriage that we should adhere to, or are we free to operate on our own understanding? Furthermore, why are some couples enjoying their union, while others are not? Finally, why do some marriages succeed while so many others fail? These are all questions that undoubtedly plague the human mind when deliberating the decision of marriage — questions, to which we will invariably need answers, before saying, I do.

Marriage is defined by the Merriam-Webster Dictionary as "the state of being united to a person of the opposite sex as husband or wife in a consensual and contractual relationship recognized by law". It is the ultimate commitment between a man and a woman. Marriage was first initiated by God in the Garden of Eden, when He brought the first woman, Eve, to the first man, Adam. That means, marriage is God's idea, and we know that anything that originates from Him is good and perfect.

Every good gift and every perfect gift is from above, and cometh down from the Father of lights, with whom is no variableness, neither shadow of turning. ***James 1:17 (KJV)***

Unfortunately, many couples, within our society today, are not enjoying marriage, and many regret ever making the decision to marry.

One of the fundamental reasons for this is lack of preparation. We spend years preparing for a career by attending college, reading books and taking examinations, but, give a lifelong decision like marriage scant regard. Seemingly, it is because of the paradigm we have that we already know what to do to have a successful marriage, because of what we have observed around us or seen on television. However, observation alone is insufficient. For instance, observing a pilot flying a plane for twenty or thirty years, does not translate to you being able to do the same without any formal training. There are a lot of principles that a pilot has to adhere to, that observation alone will not make you privy to. Likewise, watching someone drive a car for years does not mean that you will have good success if you go around the steering wheel. In both cases, crashing is more likely the end result. This is pretty much what is happening with a lot of marriages today, they are failing, because of lack of preparation.

A second reason, why many marriages are failing today is lack of knowledge. Success in life is not by accident. It is directly related to what you know. For instance, persons who know more about health, wealth or their chosen profession, tend to be more successful in those areas, than those who don't. The same is true for marriages; persons who acquire all the knowledge they can about marriage and have a deeper understanding of God's original intent for it, tend to have more success in marriage than those who do not. It is Kofi Annan who said, "Knowledge is power. Information is liberating." Persons who have divorced, will attest to the fact that, had they known better, they would have done better.

This book is designed to help you prepare for and increase your knowledge of marriage. It is based on principles from the Bible. It is your instructor's manual that will ensure that you leave the runway smoothly, avoid crashes, reduce turbulence and enjoy a happy and successful marriage. It delves into critical issues affecting marriages, such as: finance, communication, unrealistic expectations and purpose. If you imbibe the principles in this book and apply it to your preparation for marriage, you will be well on your way to good results.

CHAPTER 1

Choosing the Right Mate

According to the American Psychological Association, about 40 to 50 percent of marriages in the United States end in divorce[i]. The same is true for many other developed nations, with countries like England and Wales reporting an estimated 42 percent of marriages ending in divorce (Office for National Statistics, 2011)[ii]. In addition, many developing nations have also reported a rise in the number of divorces. It stands to reason therefore, that marriage must be approached with much diligence and preparation to avert having the same result.

Perhaps, one of the most important and fundamental principles to alleviate divorce, is to make sure that you choose the right mate. In construction, the foundation of a building is most critical. If the foundation is poorly laid, then the collapsing of that building is inevitable. The same is true for marriages. If the foundation (which in this case refers to the chosen mate) is faulty, it is unlikely that you will be able to build a long and lasting relationship, as sooner or later, you will begin to feel the rumblings under your feet.

This has been the experience of many married couples. Experts have also concurred that many couples, within a few months of tying the knot regret their decision, when the delightful honeymoon stage is over, the reality stage kicks in and masks are removed. That is when they, for the first time, meet the real person they wedded. Regrettably, this real person is oftentimes opposite their ideal of a mate. At this juncture, they are faced with only two options, to stay in the marriage despite their disappointment or divorce and try again. Many opt for the latter, only to find the cycle repeated. Statistics show that 60 to 67 percent of second marriages and 70 to 73 percent of third marriages in America end in divorce[iii].

Thankfully, this does not have to be your story. You can significantly reduce the likelihood of divorce by applying the guidelines available within

God's Word that are designed to help you to discern the right mate. Below are some of these guidelines:

GENERAL GUIDELINE

Do not be unequally yoked.

In the Old Testament, the nation of Israel was given a clear directive not to intermarry with foreign nations. Deuteronomy 7:3, "*Do not intermarry with them. Do not give your daughters to their sons or take their daughters for your sons*" (NIV). God re-emphasized this guideline under the New Covenant in 2 Corinthians 6:14 which states, "*Be ye not unequally yoked together with unbelievers: for what fellowship hath righteousness with unrighteousness? and what communion hath light with darkness?*" (KJV). Any true believer in Christ will find it very difficult to have intimate fellowship with someone who is an unbeliever, because spiritually they are from two different worlds (light and darkness). Even if you have similar interests presently, guaranteed as you grow in Christ, your interests will become increasingly dissimilar. You will find yourself increasingly interested in the things of God, while your partner's interest will be in the things of this world, and the Bible admonishes us that two cannot walk unless they agree (Amos 3:3). Consequently, any believing man or woman who is desirous of being married must seek a mate that is a part of the family of God.

GUIDELINES FOR MEN

Help meet

*The LORD God said, "It is not good for the man to be alone. I will make a helper suitable for him." **Genesis 2:18 (NIV)***

Every man, desirous of marriage, should seek for a woman who is gifted and equipped with the grace to aid him in his God ordained assignment and purpose in the earth. According to the scriptures, God made Eve to be a helper (assistant) who was suitable for Adam (Genesis 2:18). That means, she had all the qualities and complementary skills to assist him in fulfilling his mandate of taking dominion over the earth (Gen 1:26). If the woman you desire to marry lacks the competence or the potential to help you fulfill your mandate, then it stands to reason that she is not your ideal mate.

Undoubtedly, marrying a woman who is not your help meet will cause much frustration within the marriage. You will find yourself trying to coerce her to becoming just that (your help meet), even if it is not her natural inclination or calling. A pastor may, for instance, desire a wife that preaches and as such forces his wife to do so, and a business man may desire a wife that can assist him with the books. This will inevitably lead to quarrels and a falling-out between both parties, as human beings despise when you try to change them into someone else. Moreover, your frustration could lead you to seeking help externally, which can easily open the door to extramarital affair. How often have we heard of infidelity between a husband and his secretary who is actively assisting him with his vision and goals? For this reason, you want to make sure that you are uniting with your help meet, someone who can assist you in fulfilling your assignment in the earth.

Woman of Virtue

" Who can find a virtuous wife? For her worth is far above rubies" **Proverbs 31:10 (NKJV)**

A man's right mate is a woman who is virtuous. A virtuous woman is someone who is honest, honorable, principled and righteous (see Proverbs 31). She is also someone that can be trusted. As stated in Proverbs 31:11, *"The heart of her husband doth safely trust in her, so that he shall have no need of spoil"*(KJV). She is not easily discerned or discovered. Importantly, she cannot be discerned through natural senses, but she has to be spiritually discerned.

In simple terms, spiritual discernment is obtaining directive from the Holy Spirit concerning a decision that you must make. It is acquired through the prayer of faith. The scripture records king Solomon's prayer for discernment in 1 Kings 3:7–9 *"Now, LORD my God, you have made your servant king in place of my father David. But I am only a little child and do not know how to carry out my duties. Your servant is here among the people you have chosen, a great people, too numerous to count or number. So give your servant a discerning heart to govern your people and to distinguish between right and wrong. For who is able to govern this great people of yours?"*(NIV).

This discernment allowed the king to identify the mother of a child after two women claimed him as their own (1 Kings 3:16–28). He could not have made such a critical decision with his natural senses because there was nothing to distinguish between the two women. Both seemed sincere, but the king's reliance on God allowed wisdom to flow through him, so that the right decision could be made. In the same way, you must rely on discernment when trying to find a virtuous woman. You cannot afford to work with chance or look at the outward appearance, because only God knows the heart (1Samuel 16:7).

Submissive To Authority

" But there is one thing I want you to know:
The head of every man is Christ, the head of woman
is man, and the head of Christ is God".
1 Corinthians 11:3 (NLT)

When seeking your ideal mate, you should look for a woman who is submissive to authority. Women who cannot submit to the authorities that are in their lives presently, will have challenges submitting to their husbands. The bible states clearly in Ephesians 5:22–33 *"Wives, submit yourselves to your own husbands as you do to the Lord. For the husband is the head of the wife as Christ is the head of the church, his body, of which he is the Savior. Now as the church submits to Christ, so also wives should submit to their husbands in everything"* (NIV). A marriage is therefore out of divine order, when the woman is not submissive to her husband.

An example, in the Word, that shows the disadvantage of marrying a woman who is not submissive, is found in the book of 1 Kings. The king of Israel, Ahab, married the daughter of the king of the Sidonians, Jezebel. He was passive, laid-back and irresponsible, but Jezebel was controlling and pretty much called-the-shots within the marriage. The result was a nation that turned their backs on their God to the worship of Ashtoreth and Baal because of the queen's influence (see 1 Kings 16 – 22).

Woman of Peace

"Better to live on a corner of the roof than share a house with a quarrelsome wife"
Proverbs 25:24 (NIV)

The right mate for a man is a woman who is not envious and quarrelsome *"For where envying and strife is, there is confusion and every evil work"* (James 3:16, KJV). There is probably nothing more painful to a married man, than a home where there is no peace. This is certainly one of the reasons why so many married men find somewhere to hang out after work, refusing to go straight home. A man's home should be a place of tranquility, where he is able to rejuvenate to face the challenges of the next day. If all he comes home to is strife and a vile environment, the rejuvenating becomes impossible.

GUIDELINES FOR WOMEN

Leave And Cleave

"...For this cause shall a man leave father and mother, and shall cleave to his wife: and they twain shall be one flesh?" **Matthew 19:5 (KJV)**

Before saying, I do, a woman should be certain that her prospective mate is willing to both leave his parents and cleave unto her. A man who is unwilling to leave and cleave will make an irresponsible husband, one that is immature and not ready to assume the role of leader in his household. Therefore, before accepting a man's proposal, find out how close he wants to live to his parents, and how often he needs to visit them. These are telltale signs. A man who cannot conceive living a mile away from his parents, and who finds the thought of not seeing them on a weekly basis inconceivable, is likely one that is not willing to leave and cleave. Sooner or later, his parents will have too much of an influence in everything that goes on in that marriage. You will never mature as a couple and learn to make decisions on your own when parents have so much influence in your decision-making.

Purpose-Driven

An indicator of a man that would make a good husband, is one who knows his purpose and is walking in that purpose. A man without a purpose is like a ship without a compass or sail. He has no sense of direction or desired destination and will just continue to go around in circles. Moreover, you will be taken along with him on this journey to nowhere. Therefore, the first question that you should ask any man who desires for you to be his wife, is what is your purpose? If he cannot tell you definitively, then he is not ready for marriage. The last thing you want is for your spouse to discover his purpose late in the marriage and then drag you on a mission you did not bargain for.

Grace For His Calling

"But don't begin until you count the cost. For who would begin construction of a building without first calculating the cost to see if there is enough money to finish it?" **Luke 14:28 (NLT)**

A third guideline, for a woman seeking to identify her ideal mate, is that she should only join herself to a man she has the capacity, willingness and grace (divine enablement) to support with his assignment. Failure to do so could result in significant problems for the marriage. Moses' wife

Zipporah, for example, had to release her husband to fulfill his assignment as deliverer of the people of Israel. Think of how difficult it must have been for her, knowing that his assignment required her to move from her homeland to live in a foreign land with a people that were being held captive. Moreover, he was a fugitive from that land. Think also of how difficult it must have been for her to accept the fact that his assignment would involve him leaving the family for weeks at a time, as he did when he went to Mount Sinai to fast for 40 days and nights. She must have had the grace to support him with such a great call.

In the same vein, you must have the grace as a wife for your husband's assignment. When your prospective mate reveals his assignment to you, ask yourself this question , is this something that I have the grace for? Oftentimes women are quick to marry men of God with great assignments, not recognizing the cost that comes with the call. They then become extremely frustrated as they do not have the grace or capacity to deal with the price their husband has to pay. It is only prudent therefore, that you make sure you are his right match, before saying, I do.

Improving Your Value

A woman's ideal mate is a man who loves and adds value to her life. Ephesians 5:25–28 states, " *Husbands, love your wives, even as Christ also loved the church, and gave himself for it; That he might sanctify and cleanse it with the washing of water by the word, That he might present it to himself a glorious church, not having spot, or wrinkle, or any such thing; but that it should be holy and without blemish. So ought men to love their wives as their own bodies. He that loveth his wife loveth himself* " (KJV).

This passage of scripture is letting you know that as Jesus is to the church, one who loves, edifies and builds it up, so should your ideal mate be for you. So be very careful of men who tear you down with their words, rather than build you up. The husband God has for you will be able to see your potential and unearth the greatness that is within you. So, when a man courts you, look for these telltale signs. Life is too short to marry a pessimist.

As someone who is planning on getting married, endeavor to follow these guidelines and apply them to your life, so that you can receive the person God has for you. That way your marriage will bring you happiness and joy and the likelihood of living in regret will be minimal.

CHAPTER 2

God's Approval

"Only I can tell you the future before it even happens......". Isaiah 46:10a (NLT)

There are many believers who are of the opinion that we should choose our mate without including God in the decision making process. But should we accept this philosophy, when so many Christian marriages end in divorce? A survey conducted by the Barna Research Group in the United States showed that 33 and 26 percent of Born-again Christians and Evangelicals, respectively, have been divorced (Barna Group, Ltd 2008)[iv]. These figures indicate that marrying someone of the same faith is not the only ingredient required for a successful marriage.

It is essential that you have God's approval, as it will decrease the likelihood of your marriage having the same fate.

Interestingly, in our society today, many believers are relying on alternative sources to assist them in finding their ideal mate. An increasingly popular source is the online dating websites that promise to find a person's best match based on compatibility. Some of these sites have garnered millions of members; one has even been dedicated to matching Christian singles.

Undoubtedly, technology is great and can be used to help us to make informed decisions, but is it the best source when making a destiny decision? Clearly not; God is the only one who can connect you with the one who will compliment you at the most intricate levels of your being (spirit, soul and body). In fact, He knows every detail of your life, even the latent potential that you yourself are ignorant of. When He does the matching, all of these things are undoubtedly taken into consideration. Additionally, you should be aware that dating websites are merely computer programs that match individuals using the information inputted. Therefore, "garbage in, garbage out" (GIGO). Falsified information can be added, and in that case, you may be matched with someone who is completely opposite your ideal of a mate. As a matter of fact, a serial rapist used one of the popular dating websites to prey on unsuspecting victims in the United States in 2013, which proves the unreliability of this source.

A second cultural practice among Christians today is to date around until they find their Mr. or Mrs. Right. Regrettably, this method has led many to a number of heartbreaks and inescapably low self-esteem issues, stemming from the unwholesome relationships they developed through serial dating.

Another practice of some persons, is to rush into marriage because of the philosophy they adhere to that says Mr. or Mrs. Right is someone who treats you right and says "I love you" a few times. But is that really enough? Should you really get married to someone just because they say I love you and you believe you love them? As straightforward and convincing as that may appear, many have gone down that road, only to discover that their partner's real motive for marriage was money, prestige, sex, security or to solve their loneliness problem. Also, many today, though they say they love, do not know its true meaning. That is why it is imperative to ascertain God's will before saying, I do.

You must recognize that choosing your mate is not like choosing the car of your dreams, the food that you eat or clothes that suit you perfectly. Those decisions are mundane and are not destiny decisions. They are trivial and inconsequential to your purpose, and are generally chosen based on your own preferences or inhibitions. So, if you bought the wrong car, wore the wrong outfit to an event or ordered food that taste horrible, they would have no effect on your destiny. You can easily bounce back and correct those inconsequential choices.

It is quite the contrary however, when it comes to choosing your life partner, because this person is now joined to you as one flesh. That means, they can pretty much make you or break you. They can either help you to succeed or hinder you from achieving your life's purpose. The Bible tells us the story of Delilah, Samson's Philistine girlfriend, who had such an influence on him that she convinced him to tell the secret of his strength (see Judges 16). A decision that ultimately led to his death. Imagine how much more of an influence she would have had on him if she was his wife? Samson's experience shows us that we cannot treat a decision about marriage at the same level as the routine decisions that are made every day; God's approval must be sought.

Below are some tips that serve as a guide to help you to obtain God's direction concerning a prospective spouse.

Prayerfully Seek God's Will

God's directive can be derived by prayerfully seeking His will. The scripture says, *"In all your ways acknowledge Him, And He shall direct your paths"* Proverbs 3:6 (NKJV). If you go before God and make your request known, that you are believing Him for direction concerning a prospective spouse, then you will begin to see His invisible hand directing your path.

Abraham's servant, for example, when He was sent on a mission to find a wife for Abraham's son Isaac, prayed that God would direct him to the right mate for him. Before he was finished praying, the scripture says, Rebecca came to the well at which he stood and carried out everything according to his prayer (see Genesis 24). He had a successful mission because he trusted the Lord for direction.

Know God's Voice

Become acquainted with the way God communicates with you. There is a dominant way in which God speaks to all of His children. For some, He speaks in visions, to others, in dreams; for some He uses impressions, while others hear His still small voice. The scripture is replete with many examples of this. For instance, Joseph, Jesus' father after the flesh received directive concerning God's will repeatedly through dreams, which means that was his dominant way of hearing God's voice. There is a greater assurance that comes to your spirit when you know you have heard God's voice. So think about the dominant way God has spoken to you over the years. That way, when he shows you His will concerning your spouse, you will have no doubt as to His choice.

"As he considered this, an angel of the Lord appeared to him in a dream. "Joseph, son of David," the angel said, "do not be afraid to take Mary as your wife. For the child within her was conceived by the Holy Spirit. And she will have a son, and you are to name him Jesus, for he will save his people from their sins."
Matthew 1: 20–21 (NLT)

"After the wise men were gone, an angel of the Lord appeared to Joseph in a dream. "Get up! Flee to Egypt with the child and his mother," the angel said. "Stay there until I tell you to return, because

Herod is going to search for the child to kill him."
Matthew 2: 13 (NLT)

"When Herod died, an angel of the Lord
appeared in a dream to Joseph in Egypt. "Get up!"
The angel said. "Take the child and his mother back
to the land of Israel, because those who were trying
*to kill the child are dead." **Matthew 2: 19 (NLT)***

God's Peace

Look to see if you have God's peace about the person you desire to marry. If there is no peace, then chances are God is not in it. God's peace is the inner witness of the Spirit, a further confirmation, that God gives each of His children as an endorsement of His will. Proceeding with a relationship where there is an uneasiness or disturbance in your spirit, will prove detrimental in the future, even when everything in the natural makes sense. God always sees something you don't, and as a responsible Father, He will cause discomfort in your spirit in an attempt to stop you from making a wrong choice.

Having God's approval is one of the distinguishing marks of a Christian marriage. Just knowing that God has endorsed your relationship will give you the faith to stand. It is very unlikely that you will opt to divorce and remarry; if you are certain that the person you wedded was God's will for your life. Why settle for a marriage where you are always second guessing yourself, wondering if you made the right decision. Make the choice to ascertain God's approval and you will be more confident in the decision you have made concerning your mate.

CHAPTER 3

The Bait

"Be anxious for nothing, but in everything by prayer and supplication, with thanksgiving, let your requests be made known to God; and the peace of God, which surpasses all understanding, will guard your hearts and minds through Christ Jesus"
Philippians 4:6–7 (KJV)

Have you ever been too quick to make a decision that you ended up regretting immensely, because you made the wrong choice? All good decisions require time and careful consideration. Before making any decision, it is prudent that you ask yourself some questions. For example, does this line up with my values? Is it the right thing to do? How will it impact those around me? What are the pros and cons? Is this practical or nonsensical? Is this taking me to my desired destination?

As with every decision, the choice of a mate requires careful and prayerful consideration. This is why a Christian single should never become anxious when choosing his/her mate, because anxiety will open the door for Satan to bait you with the wrong person.

Satan knows that there is generally a waiting period before God releases a suitable mate to those who are praying and believing, because He is a God of timing. The bible affirms this by saying *"There is a time for everything, and a season for every activity under the heavens"* Ecclesiastes 3:1 (NIV). Unfortunately, believers have a tendency to waver in their faith during this period of waiting, becoming anxious and frustrated. This anxiety provides the perfect opportunity for the enemy to send an ill-suited and incompatible person their way, knowing very well that people will generally bite the bait and compromise their standards for an immediate gratification. Many female believers will attest to the fact that they allowed the thought of being single and childless indefinitely to overwhelm them; so they married without doing their due diligence. So, instead of marrying a Boaz, their impatience led them to marrying a Bozo.

Importantly, acting outside of God's timing never produces good results. Abraham, for example, was one of the greatest men of faith in the bible, but his anxiety led him to produce an illegitimate child, Ishmael (see Genesis 16). Had he come to that place of rest and simply wait on God's timing, he would have seen that situation for what it really was — Satan's bait.

Thankfully, you can avoid the pitfall of the enemy's bait if you make Philippians 4:6–7 your daily routine. Once you remain prayerful and continue to give God thanks on a daily basis for what you are believing Him for, then His peace that passes all human understanding will protect your heart from fears and anxiety. However, if you fail to appropriate that peace, you will never enter God's rest and you will become a victim of Satan's schemes. This is what the bible affirms in Hebrews 4:11 that says, *"Let us labour therefore to enter into that rest, lest any man fall after the same example of unbelief "*(KJV).

In like manner, you can avoid the enemy's deception by being resolute that you will not compromise your Godly principles and values to get married. If you stand firm in what you know to be just and true, then Satan cannot easily lure you to bite his bait, if your stance is evident that you are not open to any form of compromise. It is when you are not firmly rooted in your beliefs that he is able to entice you to lower your standards to get married. We know the story of King Solomon well. He was the wisest man on earth and he knew God's statutes; yet, Satan was able to entice him to marry women of foreign nations who worshiped pagan gods because he was not firmly rooted in his belief (1 Kings 11:1). He ended up sinning against God and was ultimately judged because he was lured away to pagan worship by these wives (see 1 Kings 11).

You must always be mindful that Satan is a deceiver. The bible calls him *"the one deceiving the world"* in Revelation 12:9 (NLT). As such, you must not be unaware of his schemes (2 Corinthians 2:11b). He will do anything to lure you away from the mate God has for you, even by baiting you with someone who is 'good'. You should know though that there is a difference between a good mate and a 'God mate'. A God mate is someone who compliments you in your assignment and purpose in the earth, whilst a good mate is someone who has great qualities, but is not wired to do so. Accordingly, as one who is looking to get married, always be mindful that the counterfeit generally comes before the genuine. If you have that mindset, then you will not be quick to marry the first person who looks like marriage material. You will take your time to diligently assess the person to see if they are in line with God's will for your life. In the same way that it does not take much to get a ship off course, it does not take much to derail, delay or abort your purpose; it just takes one bad decision.

Certainly, because of the times we are living in, it is very difficult to stand firm in what you believe, because the world is increasingly imposing its liberal views on the church. What is encouraging however, is that God promises in His word that "*but as people sinned more and more, God's wonderful grace became more abundant*" (Romans 5:20, NLT). If you plug into the grace of God through prayers, fasting and the study of the Word, then that grace will rest upon you and you will be able to stand firm until you receive the one God has for you.

CHAPTER 4

The Importance of Purpose in Marriage

Everything God created and every decision He makes, is done with purpose in mind. For instance, mankind's existence today would not have been possible, or would have been extremely difficult if the sun, moon, earth, sea, water, vegetation, plants, fish, animals, oxygen and so on were not functioning according to the purpose for which they were created.

Purpose can be defined as the reason or intention for which something is done or created. Therefore, when God created marriage, He had purpose in mind. Unfortunately, many believers marry without first discovering God's purpose for marriage, and as a result, God's original intent is not being fulfilled through many unions today.

To this end, the following is recommended before saying, I do.

Discover the Purpose of Marriage

Be conscious that God has a purpose for your marriage. If you go into marriage ignorant and neglectful of this fact, you will start your marriage off on the wrong footing, and you will end up pursuing your own objectives, rather than God's. That is why some couples fail to see God's blessings in their marriage; they have not learned to put first things first (Matthew 6:33). God will take care of your business when you take care of His. It is the law of sowing and reaping.

The Purpose of Marriage

So what then is the purpose of marriage? Is it to have a partner who will follow you on excursions around the world? Is it to have children and by extension grandchildren or to find someone who will solve your loneliness problem? Certainly not! From a biblical perspective, marriage is an institution through which God establishes His kingdom in the earth. This precedence was established when He brought the first couple, Adam and Eve, together and gave them their assignment of taking dominion over all the earth.

And God said, Let us make man in our image, after our likeness: and let them have dominion over the fish of the sea, and over the fowl of the air, and over the cattle, and over all the earth, and over every creeping thing that creepeth upon the earth.
Genesis 1:26 (KJV)

Avoid Conflicting Calls

Avoid marrying someone whose purpose conflicts with yours; but rather seek to marry someone whose call complements yours. For a marriage to fulfill God's original intent, both partners must have calls that are congruent. That means, your partner's call cannot be pulling them east while your call is pulling you west, that is division. Jesus makes it very clear in Mark 3:25 that "*if a house is divided against itself, that house cannot stand*" (NIV). This is why so many Christian couples end up divorcing, because their assignments were taking them in completely different directions and two can only walk together when they agree (Amos 3:3). Notably, non-Christian couples, whose pursuit in life complements each other, will have greater success in their marriage than Christian couples whose pursuits conflicts.

Uncover Motive

People are more inclined to marry for the wrong reasons when purpose is not at the forefront of their union. Sex, friend and family pressures, financial security, and aging are all factors that can lead a person to marry. The end result of many of these marriages however, is divorce, because there is no depth to the union. A marriage needs solid and significant reasons to be successful, and purpose provides that significance as it gives you God's perspective on the matter rather than yours or man's.

Be Mindful of Abuse and Misuse

It is Dr. Myles Munroe who said, "when purpose is not known, abuse is inevitable". If you get married without knowing the purpose of the marriage, then without doubt you will abuse and misuse your spousal relationship. Likewise, you and your spouse will mistreat each other if you have no idea why each person exists. You will end up saying and doing things that negate the call of God on your partner's life, which equates to abuse and misuse.

For example, a husband may put down his wife in the area of her calling as a missionary and vice versa, because they are ignorant of their partner's assignment in the earth.

Live with the consciousness that everything God gives us and everything He creates is for a reason or intention, including marriage. Discover the purpose of marriage today, and use your prospective partner's assignment as a gauge to see if your calls are congruent. Also, ensure that you both have the correct motive for marriage so that you do not end up abusing each other. Aim to make your marriage God-centered so that you will be able to fulfill God's original intent for your union.

CHAPTER 5

Maintaining your Relationship with God

Your relationship with God is one of the first things that is likely to be affected by your new union. That is why the Apostle Paul admonished the Corinthian brethren with these words:

"An unmarried man is concerned about the Lord's affairs—how he can please the Lord. But a married man is concerned about the affairs of this world—how he can please his wife— and his interests are divided. An unmarried woman or virgin is concerned about the Lord's affairs: Her aim is to be devoted to the Lord in both body and

spirit. But a married woman is concerned about the affairs of this world—how she can please her husband. I am saying this for your own good, not to restrict you, but that you may live in a right way in undivided devotion to the Lord" **1 Corinthians 7:32–35(NIV).**

There are a lot of singles who love God and have a close relationship with Him, but after they get married, they are unable to balance their lives in such a way that God still gets preeminence. This is what Apostle Paul saw, why he forewarned those who would get married of this impending danger and the need to make sure that their relationship with God is maintained.

There are several reasons why it is important to maintain your relationship with God after marriage. First, if the devil sees that you are weak in your relationship with God, after saying, I do, there will be no end to the amount of attacks he will be able to successfully bring against your union. Bickering and fighting, without a cause, is one of his frequent attacks on couples. Also, separation and divorce without any logical reason. When you build a strong relationship with your Heavenly Father though (through prayer), the devil cannot do as he pleases with your marriage. He has to go through God first, to get to you. God's protection is always guaranteed to those who are in close fellowship with Him.

The bible tells the story of King Abimelech of Gerar, who could not touch Sarah, Abraham's wife, even though it was in ignorance that he was seeking to take her as his own; *"Indeed you are a dead man because of the woman whom you have taken, for she is a man's wife"* (Genesis 20:3, NKJV). Similarly, the Amalekites, enemies of King David, were not successful when they took David's wives as captives. Their abduction was short-lived, because God empowered his servant to not only recover his two wives, but the wives and children of all those that came under his covering. This example, is testament to the fact that David was disciplined in his relationship with God and God was there for him, when he needed Him most.

Second, maintaining your relationship with God ensures that you are spiritually strong to stand against any likely or unlikely challenge that may occur at the start of the marriage. Too often Christian couples, or one partner within the marriage quits at the beginning of their marriage. When faced with challenges, such as, the death of a loved one, in-laws, finances, child rearing, and health issues, many cave in. They are like the man who built his house upon the sand *"And the rain descended, and the floods came, and the winds blew, and beat upon that house; and it fell: and great was the fall of it"* (Matthew 7:27 KJV). Importantly, when your marriage is built on prayer, you are like the man who built his house upon the rock where *"the rain descended, and the floods came, and the winds blew, and beat upon that house; and it fell not: for it was founded upon a rock"* (Matthew 7:25 KJV). This will only be possible though when you and your spouse make the decision to carry an active prayer life into the marriage.

Third, you are more certain to get directions from God, which is extremely beneficial to making good decisions, when your relationship with God is maintained. Good decisions could be the difference between having a successful marriage and a disastrous one. It could be the difference between starting off the marriage on the right or wrong footing. Moreover, maintaining your relationship with God ensures that your purpose is not aborted. A lot of couples when they were single were doing great things for God, but after saying, I do, they only do great things for their spouse. This is why Apostle Paul wanted everyone to remain single like he was, because he knew how easy it is for persons to lose focus as to why God called them in the first place, when marriage takes center stage in their lives.

Another advantage of maintaining your relationship with God after marriage is that you will not fall into temptation so easily. One of the things Jesus told His disciples was to *"Watch and pray that ye enter not into temptation"* (Matthew 26:41a, KJV). A lot of couples have fallen prey to numerous types of temptation after marriage, for example, financial, sexual and addictions, because their relationship with God dwindled. It is unlikely that it will be any different for you if your relationship with God is not your top priority after saying, I do.

The key to preventing a similar fate first starts with you ensuring that you have a habitual prayer life before marriage. The reason for this is because habits are next to impossible to break and as such, you will do whatever it takes to maintain your life of prayer when it becomes a habit. Forming habits vary for different persons. Notwithstanding studies show that it may take from as little as 18 days up to 8 months to form a new habit. Consistency is therefore the key, if you want to maintain your relationship with God. Start by setting a specific time to pray every day; after the habit is formed, then you can be more flexible.

Second, you and your prospective spouse should agree to keep each other accountable after marriage. The scripture says in Ecclesiastes 4:9-10 *"two people are better off than one, for they can help each other succeed. If one person falls, the other can reach out and help. But someone who falls alone is in real trouble"* (NLT). Also, you can make the decision before going into marriage that after saying, I do, you will have set times that you will meet together as a couple to have times of prayer. This will help both of you to grow together as a couple as well as allow you to enjoy the benefits that the prayer of agreement brings.

*"Again I say unto you, That if two of you shall agree on earth as touching any thing that they shall ask, it shall be done for them of my Father which is in heaven". **Matthew 18:19 (KJV)***

As much as your spouse is a gift from God, you should not let anything or anyone take His place in your life. That is idolatry. Make the decision therefore, that you will apply these keys to your life, so that after marriage, God will still be Lord of your life.

CHAPTER 6

Breaking Addictions

Have you ever considered the impact of addictions on marriage? Are you aware that carrying personal addictions into a marriage can wreak havoc on the union? Addiction can be defined as any compulsive engagement in an activity (for example, gambling, gaming, smoking, shopping, masturbation and pornography) or the dependency on, craving for or enslavement to a particular substance (for example alcohol, prescription drugs and food). If it is not dealt with before you say, I do, it will gnaw at your relationship like a disease until nothing is left of it.

Several studies have shown the impact of addictions on marriage. Research conducted by the National Institute on Alcoholism and Drug Dependence in the United States, for instance, revealed that marriages in which only one spouse is a heavy drinker, were 50% more likely to end in divorce (Caba, 2013)[v]. Another showed that pornography and gaming addiction was a factor in 56% and 15% of divorces, respectively[vi]. Studies also reveal that marriages in which only one partner possessed some form of addiction were more likely to end in divorce and the reason is clear. Addictions will put a strain on any relationship, not only an emotional strain, but also financial, because money is needed to fund it, and physical, because an addict may become abusive.

Let us look at some scenarios that show the impact of addictions on a marital relationship.

Scenario 1 — Imagine a woman married to a man with a sex addiction. Think of the emotional suffering she will endure knowing that her husband is compulsively engaged in sexual relations with others. That wife will find it hard to trust her husband, because there is no end to what he will do to fulfill his addiction. Moreover, her need as a wife for love and affection will be redirected to the ones who satisfy his constant craving. Also, money that should be used to improve the overall wellbeing of his family is diverted to pay for his exploits, which inadvertently exposes his wife to the possibility of contracting sexually transmitted diseases.

Scenario 2 — Imagine a wife addicted to prescription drugs. A person who is addicted to prescription drugs can develop anxiety and bipolar disorder, as well as become schizophrenic. Think of the strain these disorders would put on the relationship, as it would be hard for any husband to deal with a wife who is always fearful and apprehensive and whose mood swings constantly.

Scenario 3 — Envision another scenario where a husband secretly struggles with an alcohol addiction. Overtime he could grow to become abusive, not only to his wife, but also his children. The family would also likely face financial woes, because as is the case with most addictions, money is needed to fund it. The fact that many evangelicals today are increasingly changing their views about the drinking of alcohol, could lead to more Christian marriages experiencing alcoholism in the future, as it becomes more socially acceptable to drink.

These scenarios show that the issue of

addiction should not be taken lightly before you say, I do. It is therefore critical that you break free from any addiction you possess before entering a marriage and that you do not marry someone who you know is addicted. Here are some biblical keys that will empower you to break-free.

Admission

To break free from any addiction, you first have to admit that you have an addiction. Oftentimes people cannot overcome their addiction because they are in constant denial. They have a problem, and they know that they have one, but they keep telling themselves it is not that bad or I can stop when I want to. Once you own-up to your addiction, the motivation to break free will follow. However, the drive will not be there to make the necessary lifestyle changes or to seek the help required, if this first step is not taken.

Renew Your Mind

One of the tendencies of human beings is to take care of the things we perceive to have value and to destroy the ones that do not. Consequently, in order to break free from addictions you must have a good image of yourself. If you know your true worth and value, it is quite unlikely that you will destroy yourself and those around you with addictions. Take the time to renew your mind with the word of God until you begin to see yourself the way God sees you. *"And be not conformed to this world: but be ye transformed by the renewing of your mind, that ye may prove what is that good, and acceptable, and perfect, will of God"*. Romans 12:2 (KJV)

Fasting

Fasting is a spiritual discipline that breaks the yoke of bondage in your life when done consistently and practiced as a lifestyle. It is one of the surest ways to deny yourself, which in turn will *"Put to death, whatever belongs to your earthly nature: sexual immorality, impurity, lust, evil desires and greed, which is idolatry"*. *Colossians 3:5 (NIV)*

Prayer

Living a habitual life of prayer will also give you grace and power you need to break free from addictions. Hebrews 4:16 admonishes us *"Let us therefore come boldly unto the throne of grace, that we may obtain mercy, and find grace to help in time of need"(KJV)*. Prayer is also a sure way of overcoming temptations; that is why Jesus advised his disciples to pray lest you enter into temptation

(Matthew 26:41). You will notice that He himself held true to this principle when He was on earth. He knew that the only way to stand firm against the temptations of the enemy was to stay in constant communion with His Heavenly Father, the giver of mercy and grace and so on many occasions He withdrew to pray (see Luke 5:16; Mark 1:35, Matthew 14:23).

Know your Triggers

Do not intentionally surround yourself with the people or go to the places that trigger your addictions. 2 Timothy 2:22 tells us to *"Flee also youthful lusts: but follow righteousness, faith, charity, peace, with them that call on the Lord out of a pure heart"* (KJV). That means, you ought to stay away from anything or anyone that will cause you to have a strong desire for the things that you are addicted to.

Humble Yourself

If you are too proud, you will never be able to break free from addictions. You have to be open to the instructions and sometimes rebuke of others. The scripture states that God sends His Word to deliver in Psalm 107:20. However, oftentimes God sends His Word through one of His servants and we are too proud to receive it. If you fail to receive the chastisement of the Lord, you will remain in bondage. That is why so many Christians come to the house of God, week after week, month after month and year after year, and remain in bondage. God sent His Word to deliver them, but their unwillingness to humbly submit to that Word, keeps them in bondage. Humbling yourself is therefore a major key to breaking free from addictions.

Seek The Help Of Others

There are different stages of addiction, and as such, a person who is at the initial stage may find it easy to overcome on their own using the principles outlined above. However, when addictions are allowed to fester and become deep-seated, that person may need to solicit the help of others to overcome. You generally know when you are at the stage where you must get help from others. When you have hit what is referred to as 'rock bottom', where you do not care about anything or anyone, including yourself, and where even the threat of incarceration no longer deters you from your addiction, you are at that stage. Seeking help from others when you can no longer help yourself is therefore a key to breaking free from addictions. The scripture underscores this concept by saying, *"Confess your faults one to another, and pray one for another, that ye may be healed. The effectual fervent prayer of a righteous man availeth much".* James 5:16 (KJV)

From this point forward, see your addictions not only as a disease that needs to be cured, but as a giant that needs to be slain and your marriage as the promise land that needs to be conquered. This giant will always stand between you and your promise land. That is why it is important that you do not see yourself as inferior to it, like the children of Israel did in Numbers 13, but like Caleb, you should see yourself as well able to conquer the land (Numbers 13:30).

Addictions should not be taken lightly when going into a marriage, because what you do not conquer will in the end conquer you. Make the decision today to start working on overcoming any addiction you may have, by applying the principles stated above. Then you will be in a better position to enjoy, keep and add value to the person God has given you.

CHAPTER 7

Money and Marriage

A recent survey, of 191 Certified Divorce Financial Analyst (CDFA), revealed that money issues was one of the top three leading causes of divorce, accounting for 22% of divorces in North America (Institute of Divorce Financial Analyst, 2013)[vii]. Another survey of people in a relationship or partnership released by Suntrust Bank showed that finances were the leading cause of stress in a relationship (Holland, 2015)[viii]. It stands to reason therefore, that good money management skills are essential, if you want a long and stress-free marriage.

Money Management refers to the control,

directing and careful handling of money. No matter how much you and your prospective spouse love each other, if money is constantly mishandled when you wed, you will unavoidably find yourself in constant arguments, that could lead to divorce.

To avert financial woes in marriage, it is a good practice to discuss finances before you say, I do. One of the first things you should discuss and discover is your prospective partner's attitude towards money. You may discover that it is completely opposite to yours. You may be a saver and your prospective spouse, a spender or vice versa. You may believe that you must save for what you want, while your prospective partner believes that you should take out a loan to get it. All these nuisances, must be worked out before marriage, so that there is less stress within the relationship.

In addition, it is important to discuss each other's financial history. You do not want to go into the marriage and have any surprises. Too often persons get married, only to discover the magnitude of debt they inherited from their spouse. Also, because each of you will have your own belief system regarding money, it is good practice to have a Christian financial counselor assist you with the discussions before marriage. In a general way though, here are some tips that will help to improve your money management skills to better prepare you to handle the finances within the marriage.

Avoid Too much Consumer Debt

Debt comes in many forms; for example, through car loans, credit cards, student loans and mortgages. It is generally acquired to purchase items that the borrower cannot afford under normal circumstances. Nowadays getting into consumer debt is quite easy with a proliferation of financial institutions offering low interest loans. If you accumulate too much consumer debt in marriage though, very soon you will feel like you are drowning in despair and hopelessness, which will have an adverse effect on your marriage.

Avoiding consumer debt requires self-control, which incidentally is one of the fruit of the Spirit (see Galatians 5:22–23). You will always be bombarded with advertisements, luring you to purchase something that you do not need and so self-control is pivotal. You must learn to be content with what you have. Being content is a sure way to avoid getting into too much debt, as it is generally persons who are discontented, who live above their means, because they are never satisfied.

Avoid Impulsive Spending

Before purchasing anything, ask yourself the question, is this a need or a want? If it is not a need, think twice before purchasing. Overspending is generally driven by our wants, rather than our needs.

Avoid Secret Spending

Secrets by themselves are enough to bring ruin to any marriage. This is especially true when the secret is tied to finances. For example, when a spouse hides to make exorbitant purchases, conflicts may arise within the marriage.

Additionally, secret spending makes it impossible for couples to work together as a team to resolve their financial issues, because teamwork requires trust and accountability, and secret spending removes both elements from the equation.

Avoid Emotional Spending

Some persons make purchases based on the mood they are in, so, they may decide to reward themselves with an expensive vacation on credit because of a major achievement, such as a promotion. Similarly, they may make costly purchases, outside of the family budget, because they feel sad. These types of emotional spending however, breaks down fiscal discipline, which is essential for maintaining fiscal health and stability within a marriage, and should be avoided.

Avoid Covetousness

"And he said unto them, Take heed, and beware of covetousness: for a man's life consisteth not in the abundance of the things which he possesseth". **Luke 12:15 (KJV)**

One of the surest ways to come to poverty is to have a covetous spirit. Covetousness is "feeling or showing a very strong desire for something that you do not have and especially for something that belongs to someone else" (Merriam-Webster dictionary). When our desire for things becomes excessive and unreasonable, we will make bad financial decisions. For example, a person who is covetous could find themselves buying a car that they cannot afford or a house that is outside of their budget, because a friend possesses those things. This is part of the reason why the bank has ended up repossessing so many cars and homes of persons who could not meet their quarterly or monthly obligations. They took the loans without first counting the costs because of covetousness. Proverbs 28:22 warns that, *"A man with an evil eye hastens after riches, And does not consider that poverty will come upon him."* (NKJV). Before saying, I do, watch out for this spirit or financial ruin will be inevitable.

Maintain a Budget

Carry the discipline of budgeting into the marriage. Budgeting refers to " making sure that you're spending less than you're bringing in and planning for both the short and long-term" (Fontinelle, unknown)[ix]. Budgeting will reduce the likelihood of you and your partner falling into a cycle of debt. It will also better position you and your spouse to achieve whatever future goals you may have. You can find one of the best free online budgeting tools to help you get started at Mint.com.

Saving and Investing

Get into the habit of saving and investing. If money is constantly being consumed, you will have nothing for the future. There are a number of savings products that are offered by commercial banks, building societies, credit unions and so on that can be explored. There are also several investment options available including stocks, bonds, real estate, business, Certificate of Deposit (CD) and commodities. After you tithe, consider using the 50/30/20 rule as a guide, where 50% of your income is put towards fixed expenses, 30% towards discretionary spending and 20% savings/investments.

Pool Your Resources

Break away from the 'my money, your money', mentality and recognize that after marriage, both of you are now one (including your finances). Couples who pool their resources together to achieve their goals and purpose do far greater and are more impactful, than couples who work as individuals. For example, deciding to have a joint account to deal with expenses could make it easy to handle the overall finances affairs of the home.

How you handle money in marriage cannot be overemphasized because money is no respecter of persons. Those who manage it well will reduce conflicts, stress and financial and relational ruin, but those who do not are doomed to a life of misery. You want to make sure, before you say, I do, that money management becomes a top priority in your life. See every day as an opportunity to improve. Then it will be unlikely, that your marriage will be torn apart, because you or your spouse are bad stewards.

CHAPTER 8

Management in Marriage

Anything that you do not manage or manage well will eventually degenerate and deteriorate. If you have a car that you drive daily, for instance, and you do not service it, that car will eventually break down and leave you on the side of the road. Even if the car is brand new, continued neglect will lead to its ruin, and you will have nothing to drive at the end of the day. The same is true for marriage; it requires management to remain sustainable.

In consequence of that, it is critical that you work on your management skills before saying, I do. A marriage encompasses the management of several things, including one's self, relationship with your spouse, children, home and so on. If you fail to manage all the elements of marriage simultaneously, something or someone will be neglected and your union will suffer for it. Even if your marriage is ordained by God, if you do not learn balance, it will be hard to retain it.

One of the greatest illustrations of this principle is found in the book of Genesis. God gave Adam the Garden of Eden and instructed him to tend it; that is to say, to manage, administer and govern it. However, Adam failed when he allowed satan to invade and penetrate his environment. Satan's invasion was so destructive, that God had no choice but to take back the garden from Adam. Adam lost his home because he failed to govern what God had entrusted to his care. (see Genesis 3:23)

Likewise, David in his failure to manage himself, which was evidently played out when he committed adultery and took the life of an innocent man, led to a total breakdown in his family. His Son Amnon for example, raped his sister Tamar and his son Absalom tried to kill him in an attempt to take over his kingdom. (see 2 Samuel 13; 2 Samuel 15 and 2 Samuel 12)

These examples are useful lessons that are

applicable in marriage, because a sustainable marriage and management are like opposite sides of the same coin; you cannot have one without the other.

The good news is that, your years of singleness are preparatory years, that must be used to develop the management skills required for your marriage and home. Here are a few tips that will assist you in this regard.

Management begins with you

Management begins with you. That means, you must first work on managing yourself, before you can manage anything or anyone around you. If you can achieve balance presently, with everything that is on your plate, you should be able to transfer that skill to anyone or anything that is added to your life.

Jesus, for example, learned personal management before He took on the twelve apostles. The bible records Him in Luke 4:4 for instance, disciplining Himself and bringing His flesh under the dominion of the Holy Spirit, through 40 days of fasting in the wilderness. The bible also shows His discipline in Mark 1:35, which records Him getting up early in the morning, while it was still dark to have fellowship with the Father. There are also a number of other scriptures that reveal Jesus as a man who managed His life, time, body and flesh. As a result, He did not lose any of the disciples God had entrusted to His care, except the Son of Perdition who was doomed for destruction (John 17:12).

Management is developed when you take personal responsibility

When you take personal responsibility, management is developed. Therefore, before you say, I do, do not shy away from responsibilities, but endeavor to take on additional ones when the opportunity arises. For example, if you are living with your parents, seek to take on one or more of the family expenses, such as paying a bill. This will prepare you for the responsibility of paying bills and help you to develop the discipline of paying them on time when you are married. Something else that you could do, is seek to do more domestic chores within the home, for example, cooking, cleaning and washing. One of the responsibilities of marriage is managing the home, so it is good to develop the skill from early. Plus, you will not have mommy or daddy around to pick up after you anymore.

Management grows when you learn to do several activities simultaneously

Management grows when you learn how to balance several activities within a particular time frame successfully. One of the surest ways to accomplish this is by creating a things to do list in the morning. This list would comprise all the important task that you want to accomplish within a 24-hour period. If you carry that discipline into your marriage, guaranteed, you will be able to manage the increased activities that you will face, especially when children come into the picture. If you fail to develop this essential discipline, you will feel overwhelmed by the responsibilities of marriage, which could lead to a breakdown of several other important areas within the union.

Management requires action

Management is more about doing, than it is about saying. Oftentimes we say, but never do; so things that are important to us never get accomplished. Becoming a more action-oriented person, however, requires discipline. One of the ways to develop this discipline is to work hard on ensuring that the things you set out to do on a daily basis are done. You can do this by grading yourself at the end of the day, to see how many items off the things to do list were accomplished. Also, you want to make sure that you accomplish the goals that you set out for yourself prior to marriage, no matter how small they are. If you take this attitude into the marriage, where the responsibilities, tasks and activities are greater, then success is inevitable, and the things that you must manage within the union, will get done. Conversely, if before getting married, you say, but rarely do, then, you will bring that habit within the union and things that are entrusted to you will breakdown under your care.

The sustainability of your marriage will largely depend on how much you improve your management skills. Do not wait until you tie the knot to try to get it all together. That may be too late. Work on yourself now, adopt the recommendations, apply them to your life while you wait to say, I do. Then you will be better prepared to handle the demands of marriage and keep what God has entrusted to you.

CHAPTER 9

Forgiveness

Unforgiveness is to a marriage what poison is to the body. If it is not dealt with, then slowly it will gnaw at the relationship, until the marriage is ruined. Unforgiveness can be defined as the unwillingness to pardon someone for a wrong done. Whether you married the right person or the wrong one, are confrontational or submissive, you will not escape having to deal with offense in marriage. How you respond to offense however, will determine the success or failure of your marriage.

Unavoidably, couples say and do things to each other (whether intentionally or unintentionally) that are insulting and even disrespectful, because they are two imperfect persons, trying to build a perfect marriage. A husband for example, may genuinely forget his wife's birthday or anniversary, maybe because he was busy with work and the pressure to meet deadlines. In consequence, his wife is offended. God forbid he forgets the next year. A seed of unforgiveness is easily planted within her heart, because he has now twice committed the 'unpardonable sin'.

Unfortunately, when a seed of unforgiveness is planted, it begins to ruin the marriage in a number of ways. First it cuts off the communication channel between spouses and without that free flow of communication, the relationship will die, because communication is to a relationship, what the blood is to the body (Leviticus 17:14). A lot of marriages are on life support today, because many couples are living in the same house, eating at the same table, sleeping in the same bed, but are not communicating. From the outside all seems well, but slowly they are dieing, because a seed of unforgiveness has eaten the life out of the union.

The second way unforgiveness ruins a marriage, follows the first. If couples are not communicating, they will likely experience a breakdown of sexual intimacy within the marriage, which is like adding fuel to a fire. Once sexual needs are not being met within the marriage, the door to infidelity could be opened, because couples tend to seek outside of their marriage, what they cannot get on the inside. That is why the bible instructs couples not to *"... deprive each other of sexual relations, unless you both agree to refrain from sexual intimacy for a limited time so you can give yourselves more completely to prayer. Afterward, you should come together again so that Satan won't be able to tempt you because of your lack of self-control"* 1 Corinthians 7:5 (NLT)

Third, unforgiveness can place the desire within a spouse's heart for revenge, because of the hurt that resulted from the offense. This could lead to a bitter back and forth between both parties, perpetuating a cycle of pain, until separation becomes the only course of action for relief. This is especially true for spouses who are not spiritually mature.

Unforgiveness will also keep anger alive within a marriage, which in turn, easily gives the enemy entrance into the union. This is why the scriptures says *"Be ye angry, and sin not: let not the sun go down upon your wrath. Neither give place to the devil"*. Ephesians 4:26–27 (KJV). Once satan has a secure position from which he can do his operations, he will cause havoc to take place within that marriage until it is ruined. He does this by sowing more seeds of discord and distrust, until the marriage falls apart.

Equally important, unforgiveness stifles an offended spouse's ability to love their partner. When a spouse decides not to forgive, their heart will eventually become cold and hard towards their partner until the person they once held nearest and dearest, becomes distant and hated. There are so many examples in our world today of combative divorce court proceedings between couples who were once crazily in love with each other. They allowed unforgiveness to grow until their love for each other waned and they had to go their separate ways.

At no point do you want to find yourself in this precarious position after marriage, so here are some keys that will prepare you to handle offenses when they come after saying, I do.

Decision

Recognize that forgiveness is a decision. This is why the scriptures instructs us to forgive (Matthew 6:14). God wants us to know that it is an act of the will and not of the emotions. Once you make the decision to forgive, His grace will be released to help you through the process of restoration.

Do Not Meditate on or Retell the Offense

After you make the decision to forgive, do not meditate on the wrong done to you, because anything you meditate on will grow. Likewise, do not keep retelling the story. Retelling will cause you to relive the experience over and over again, until you find yourself back into that place of unforgiveness. The only time you should rehearse past offenses is when it is being used as a tool to help others overcome.

Have a Positive Perspective

Having a positive outlook will help you to see the good in every negative situation. You can, for example, view offenses as something that is designed to make you better and stronger, not bitter or weaker. Once you have that mindset, offense will be your friend and not your foe. Besides, how will you know that you are spiritually mature unless offense confirms this to be so? If you get offended quite easily, it is a strong indicator that you have some growing up to do.

Seek Spiritual Help

In some cases, because of the magnitude of the

offense, or how long the offense has been allowed to fester, seeking help from someone who is at a higher level spiritually or who has gone through a similar situation can give you the courage needed to break free from unforgiveness. This is what the scripture alludes to when it says, *"Brethren, if a man be overtaken in a fault, ye which are spiritual, restore such an one in the spirit of meekness; considering thyself, lest thou also be tempted."* Galatians 6:1 (KJV).

The truth is no one is exempt from offenses and you must master the art of forgiveness before you say, I do. So make the decision today, that a part of your preparation for marriage will be to forgive those who offend you. Whenever you are offended, become like a little child, who is always quick to forgive and move on. Remember, forgiveness is a decision. You do not have to feel like it or wait until you feel like you should, to let someone go. You can make the decision the second the offense comes, that I am going to forgive this person, and then let your words and actions follow. This is why Jesus in His teaching admonishes us to forgive as much as seventy times seven within a given day (Matthew 18:21-22). Forgiveness is a choice that we have the power to make.

CHAPTER 10

Effective Communication

Effective communication is one of the most important keys to having a successful and happy marriage. All marriages are strengthened and improved by it. The converse is also true, marriages fail and worsen because of poor communication. In fact, the Huffington Post lists poor communication as the number one reason why couples separate[x]. Additionally, a survey of counseling professionals conducted by YourTango.com, confirms communication problems as the leading cause of divorce (YourTango, 2012)[xi].

Effective communication refers to the ability to express thoughts, feelings and ideas (both verbal and nonverbal), in a manner that is clearly understood by the recipient. It is the ability to discuss difficult topics, and at times opposing views with others, with little or no conflict. Anyone can share their thoughts and ideas, but not everyone can share them effectively.

Poor communication can affect a relationship in several ways. Number one, it can lead to misunderstanding. If you are an ineffective communicator, even with the best of intentions, and greatest of sincerity, you can be easily misunderstood by your spouse. The tone of your voice or body language, could come across as attacking or angry when you communicate. This could lead to arguments, because people will always react in a manner that is consistent with how they process the conversation. That is why it is often said, 'it is not what you say, but how you say it'. Sometimes you can even say what you are saying perfectly and still be misunderstood, maybe because of your partner's own paradigm. This is why a part of effective communication is to sometimes ask your partner the question, "what do you understand me to be saying?". This will bring clarity and remove the ambiguity from the conversation.

Number two, poor communication could lead to increased conflicts within the marriage, which can eventually harm the union. Almost all conflicts are the result of differences of opinions, so if couples do not know how to converse in a peaceful and respectful manner, the marriage could end up suffering as a result of it. Have you ever heard of couples, who divorced because of conflicts they can hardly remember the details of years later? They probably made a mountain out of a molehill because they were not effective communicators.

Lastly, poor communication affects team work. The scripture states in Ecclesiastes 4:9-12, *"Two are better than one; because they have a good reward for their labour"* (KJV). Poor communication however, robs spouses of the ability to work together as a team to solve problems. As a result, problems that could have been resolved within a short time, such as, a few months or years, end up taking them a lifetime to resolve.

On the contrary, effective communication leads to a deepening of intimacy and love between partners, which in turn strengthens the marital relationship. A marriage is only as strong as the effectiveness of the communication within the union. So, as husbands and wives learn how to share their innermost thoughts and feelings, and have open and honest communication, their affection for each other will grow. Also, when there is effective communication within a marriage, the household tends to run a lot more smoothly. A couple, who for example, has spent time effectively discussing the different roles and responsibilities of each partner within the union, is more likely to have a household that operates in an effective and efficient manner.

In view of the above, it is imperative that you add improving your communication skills to your preparation for marriage. Below are some general principles that will help you in this regard.

Listening

Communication is more about listening, than it is about speaking. God giving us two ears and one mouth may be an indicator that He wants us to listen twice as much as we speak. If you discipline yourself and enter each conversation as a keen listener, the likelihood that you will better understand what the other person is saying will increase. If you better understand what someone is saying, then you are better able to respond in an amicable way. Sometimes we are so preoccupied in trying to get our point across, that we do not truly take the time to hear and understand what the other person is saying, so effective communication never takes place.

Be Respectful

Often times arguments are the result of differences of opinion; we tend to get loud, boisterous and at times disrespectful when trying to get a point across. That is why it is important to practice being respectful of the opinion or judgment of others, even if you do not agree. Everyone is entitled to their own opinion or perspective, even if it is inaccurate, so their viewpoint must be respected. If you carry that attitude into your marriage, your spouse will love you for it. No one wants to feel, that what they have to say is stupid or nonsensical.

Give your Undivided Attention

Practice giving your undivided attention when entering a conversation. Too frequently persons say that they are listening, but their body language says differently. Their eyes are all over the place, and their posture says they are not interested. If you do that, no one will think you are taking them seriously or treating them respectfully. What you want to do, when someone desires to speak with you, is to stop whatever you are doing, focus on the conversation and make sure that you are looking the person in the face. This way, not only your words, but your posture will be saying, I am interested.

Be mindful of the way you speak

Be mindful that how you say something is just as important as what you say. People will not be quick to receive what you have to say, if you come across as being disrespectful and offensive. As such, it is suggested that you enter each conversation, thinking of the person in an admirable way. That way, your words and body language will align themselves with your thoughts.

Communicate out of love and respect

Often times communication is not effective because it is not coming from a position of love and respect, but rather anger, hurt and bitterness. This is why hurting people always hurt others; they speak out of their hurts rather than from a spirit of love. Therefore, you want to examine yourself when conversing with others, especially when you and the other person are not seeing eye to eye. Make sure that you are not speaking out of your anger, hurt or bitterness, but rather from a position of continued love and respect, and then communication will be more successful. This is what the scripture affirms when it says *"A soft answer turneth away wrath: but grievous words stir up anger"* Proverbs 15:1 (KJV).

Learn Gender Communication

Men and women communicate differently. Men generally communicate to solve problems or to share ideas, whereas women communicate to connect, for companionship and to build intimacy. A lot of the conflicts in marriage result from gender communication issues. For example, women who think their husbands are not listening and men who believe their wives are nagging. That is why it is important to learn gender communication. Men, do not assume that your wife needs solutions when she is communicating her problem to you. Chances are, she is communicating her problems to connect. Women, do not be overly annoyed when a man tries to solve your problem; he is wired that way. Instead help each other to understand how you communicate.

There is no strong, healthy and happy marriage without effective communication. The better you become at it, the better your marriage will be. Practice applying the principles above when entering conversations and you will improve your communication skills. Remember poor communication will lead to misunderstandings and conflicts, but effective communication will lead to deeper intimacy and love within a marriage.

CHAPTER 11

The Danger of Unrealistic Expectations

Before you say I do, you must ensure that you do not carry unrealistic expectations into the marriage, because you will be deeply disappointed when those expectations are not met. As a matter of fact, a recent national survey in the United States of America revealed that 45% of divorced couples gave unrealistic expectations as the reason for their divorce [xii].

Importantly, the way we think about marriage is influenced and shaped by several agents. These agents help to form our expectations, and are largely responsible for us having impractical and sometimes unreasonable ones. One such agent is the media, especially the movies, television shows and sitcoms that we watch. There are many who enter marriage expecting it to be like the relationships they see in movies. However, those relationships focus mainly on the ideal of uninterrupted romance and living 'happily ever after'. Of course, there is undoubtedly romance and happiness in marriage, but marriage is a lot more than that. So, do not expect your marriage to be the superficial way Hollywood portrays it. There is a lot more that happens behind the scenes than hugs and kisses.

Another agent that has been influencing our perspective of marriage, lately, is the social media. The proliferation of postings of couples traveling the world and flaunting their love online, has caused many unmarried persons to desire the same when they wed. But, what if you marry a person without those desires? Everybody is socialized differently, so you may end up marrying someone who is private. Moreover, he/she may not have a desire to travel the world or to post your love online; but, buying a home and raising a family, may be his/her top priority.

A third agent that shapes the way we think about marriage is our family. The family is the first social institution that is responsible for our socialization and as such, a lot of the values and expectations that we have formed, came by this means. A man, for example, may come from a household where his mom did everything within the home, including washing, cooking and cleaning, so, when he gets married, he has that same expectation of his wife. His wife, on the other hand, may have come from a family where it was the helper who did everything, so she may not be as domestic as his mom. Similarly, a wife may come from a family where her dad was skilled in a wide range of repairs and kept both the interior and exterior of the house in tip-top shape. So, she enters her marriage having the same expectation of her husband. Her husband, however, might have grown up in a home where they hired professionals to conduct necessary repairs, hence, he is not so inclined.

These are some of the differences that you have to deal with within a marriage. That is why it is important that you do not have unrealistic expectations going into it.

Unrealistic expectations may have several consequences on the marriage. For example, a person whose expectations are not met may become controlling, in an attempt to get their spouse to conform to their fantasy. Incidentally, whenever you try to control a person, you will face resistance, because God did not give mankind dominion over people, but over the creatures.

And God said, Let us make man in our image, after our likeness: and let them have dominion over the fish of the sea, and over the fowl of the air, and over the cattle, and over all the earth, and over every creeping thing that creepeth upon the earth.
Genesis 1:26 (KJV)

Needless to say, when there is resistance of this nature, it could open the door to arguments. Furthermore, couples could end up resenting everything their spouse does. This could also disintegrate the marriage, because no one will want to stay in a marriage where they are constantly blamed and criticized for their spouse's unhappiness. Sooner or later the environment will become too toxic for them.

Unrealistic expectations are responsible for a number of cases of depression in marriage. Some persons become depressed by the fact that what they had hoped for in marriage is not being realized. Regrettably, depression can lead to divorce. In fact, a study of married couples in the United States showed that a partner of a depressed spouse can become demoralized, angry and resentful. As a result, the divorce rate is nine times higher when one of the partners within the marriage suffers from depression (Healthy Exchange, 2013)[xiii].

Of course, not all of the cases are as extreme. Notwithstanding, it is important that you take some precautions, before marriage, to reduce the likelihood of being a victim to unrealistic expectations.

Advisably, the first and most important thing you need to do, is to discuss your expectations with your prospective spouse. With the help of a Marriage Counsellor, these expectations can be hashed out, until you both come to some form of agreement. Also, ensure that all areas are covered in the discussion, such as spiritual, physical and financial expectations; children; sex; values and convictions, to name a few.

You could also, on your own, look at the pros and cons of your expectations, whether they will do more harm than good to your marriage. You could discover that some of your expectations are selfish and are not coming from a place of love. The Bible makes it clear that love is not selfish (1 Corinthians 13:5–7). So, if your expectation is only to your benefit, you can remove it.

Another thing that you could do to reduce the probability of carrying unrealistic expectations into your marriage, is to check to see if your expectations are achievable. It might not be feasible, for example, to travel the world in the first few years of marriage or to buy a house, if both of you are already up to your necks in debt. Your expectations must be within your power to achieve; so if you realize the opposite, you probably need to take a second look at it.

As can be seen, carrying unrealistic expectations into a marriage can lead to disappointment, and disappointment will eventually open the door to several other problems within the marriage. There are a lot of couples whose marriages are falling apart, because of this issue of unrealistic expectations. Therefore, make the decision today, before you say, I do, that you will invest the time to discuss your expectations with your prospective spouse as failure to do so could prove devastating after the marriage.

CHAPTER 12

Children and Marriage

"Lo, children are an heritage of the LORD: and the fruit of the womb is his reward. As arrows are in the hand of a mighty man; so are children of the youth. Happy is the man that hath his quiver full of them: they shall not be ashamed, but they shall speak with the enemies in the gate".
Psalm 127:3-5(KJV)

There are a lot of disagreements and disputes within a marriage that result from, among other things, couples having children and wanting children. Unfortunately, a lot of couples fail to discuss this pertinent issue before saying, I do. Undoubtedly, preparation is key. Benjamin Franklin puts it this way, "by failing to prepare, you are preparing to fail".

Here then are some likely issues relating to children and marriage, that can affect the union, if they are not properly handled and discussed before saying, I do.

Infertility

The World Health Organization (WHO) defines infertility as "the inability of a sexually active, non-contracepting couple to achieve pregnancy in one year"[xiv]. According to the Centers for Disease Control and Prevention (CDC), "about 6% of married women 15–44 years of age in the United States are unable to get pregnant after one year of unprotected sex..."[xv]. Furthermore, the National Institute of Child Health and Human Development (NICHD) posited that "one-third of infertility cases are caused by male reproductive issues, one-third by female reproductive issues, and one-third by both male and female reproductive issues or by unknown factors" (NICHD, 2012)[xvi]. Further studies also show similar figures, 15% of couples after 1 year of having unprotected sex are unable to conceive, and 10% after being married for 2 years [xvii].

What is more alarming is the association between divorce and childlessness in marriage. Studies show that approximately 66% of couples who divorce were childless as opposed to 40% who had kids[xviii]. That means that infertility can create serious problems for a marriage if partners are not proactively prepared to deal with it. Before you say, I do, ask your prospective this question, what if we cannot have children? Then discuss the implications.

How soon after marriage will we start having children

There are a number of things to take into consideration, when making the decision, as to the ideal time after marriage to start having kids. For example, finances, age, motive, lifestyle and state of wellbeing. Oftentimes couples do not see eye to eye on some of these issues. A wife, for example, may want to start having children right away because of her age, whereas her husband may want to wait at least two years to 'enjoy' his wife before having children. That is why it is important to start discussing the issue before saying, I do. That way, both of you can come to some amicable agreement and alleviate conflicts afterward.

How many children will we have

The number of children to have is another area of possible contention between a couple. A husband for example, may only desire one child, whereas his wife has always dreamed of having a large family. Also, either party may have no desire for children. Consequently, this issue of number of children to reproduce must be discussed and settled before marriage.

Interval between children

How far apart to have children, can also be a point of contention between a couple, as often times partners have their own ideal as to when it's best suited to have their next child. A wife's ideal, for example, may be two to three years apart, whereas a husband's ideal may be one year. If they cannot come to some agreement, then this difference in opinion can become very unpleasant and escalate into arguments. My advice to you is to not trivialize this issue, but discuss it before you say, I do.

How to discipline children

Differences of opinion regarding discipline can also lead to conflicts in marriage. A husband for example, may believe children should be spanked when they are rude, whereas the wife may think a more contemporary approach should be used. If he persists and spanks the child, despite his wife's wishes, then she could become increasingly resentful of him. Something as simple as the discipline of children can spur quarrels and separation in a home; so, discuss the issue and come to some agreeable solution, before saying, I do.

Stepchildren

Stepchildren can be a big area of dispute in marriages, as the role of the stepparent is almost always not clearly defined. One step mom had this to say in the Huffington Post, "the greatest challenge is not usually direct conflict with the stepchildren, but rather, conflict over the parenting of the stepchildren" (Antebi, 2011)[xix.] For this reason, relationships with stepchildren are considered high risk for failure.

It is therefore imperative, that the role of the stepparent is made clear, before you say, I do. In addition, issues such as living arrangement, visitation, and so on, should all be agreed on before entering into marriage. If these issues are not properly dealt with, they could prove disastrous to your union, which has been the case for many couples with blended families.

In conclusion, addressing issues concerning children is a very important decision all couples will have to face. If it is handled carelessly and flippantly, or if it's dealt with ignorantly, then something that is designed to bring happiness and joy, will cause much frustration and pain. For this reason, you want to make sure that you look at all the likely occurrences that could pop-up in your marriage and resolve the issues before they occur. This way you will reduce the likelihood of arguments and fights that have the potential to tear your marriage apart.

CHAPTER 13

The Importance of Commitment in Marriage

Commitment is defined in the Oxford English dictionary as, "the state or quality of being dedicated to a cause, activity etc". The Merriam-Webster dictionary defines commitment as, "something pledged". Undoubtedly, one of the primary contributors to divorce in our society today is lack of commitment. In fact, phycologists from the University of California, Los Angeles (UCLA), posit that, a deeper level of commitment in marriage is a much better predictor of lower divorce rates and fewer problems in marriage. Studies have also shown the role of lack of commitment in divorce, with one showing as much as 85% of respondents citing it as the reason for their divorce.

So why is commitment such a challenge for so many couples after saying, I do? Why are so many unwilling to give their time and energy to making their marriage work?

First, it may be because some persons are going into marriage unprepared. It is next to impossible to remain committed to a relationship that you are not prepared for, spiritually, emotionally, intellectually and physically. As much as you love your spouse romantically, love alone is not enough to stay dedicated and loyal to your partner in the good times and bad. It takes a certain level of maturity that is acquired through preparation. As such, two very young persons may decide to marry because they love each other, but, since they do not have much life experience and they did not take the time to adequately prepare, they find themselves overwhelmed with the requirements that are essential to making a marriage work. Consequently, they may end up divorcing.

Second, the perception many hold could be responsible for the increasing number of persons who are entering marriage uncommitted. Many today enter marriage with the preconceived notion that it is okay to divorce when things are not going as expected within the union. That is why many celebrities sign what is called a prenuptial agreement. Even within our churches, from the clergy to the laity, are divorcing and remarrying like never before. Once you enter a marriage, with the option to divorce foremost within your mind, if things do not work out the way you expect, you will never commit fully to that relationship. This is why God in all His wisdom, only permitted divorce for sexual misconduct.

"Jesus replied, "Moses permitted you to divorce your wives because your hearts were hard. But it was not this way from the beginning"
Matthew 19:8 (NIV)

"I tell you that anyone who divorces his wife, except for sexual immorality, and marries another woman commits adultery" **Matthew 19:9 (NIV).**

Moreover, God hates divorce, so we should never enter marriage with that faulty preconception that it is okay to divorce if the marriage has challenges that we did not anticipate.

Didn't the LORD make you one with your wife? In body and spirit you are his. And what does he want? Godly children from your union. So guard

your heart; remain loyal to the wife of your youth.
"For I hate divorce!" says the LORD, the God of
Israel. "To divorce your wife is to overwhelm her
with cruelty" says the LORD of Heaven's Armies.
"So guard your heart; do not be unfaithful to your
wife" **Malachi 2: 15 -16 (NLT).**

The third reason why couples are less committed to their marriage is because they do not esteem and value their union. Anything we value in life, we give ourselves and attention to. This has been one of the main reasons why ministers who put their ministry above their marriage end up losing their spouse, because most of their dedication and devotion went to their ministry at the expense of their marriage.

Additionally, the lack of commitment in marriage is as a result of some persons going into marriage without a 'commitment mind-set'. That is to say, persons who cannot commit to anything or anyone in their lives, before marriage, will carry that same uncommitted mind-set into the union. As soon as they get bored or feel challenged, they will move on to the next relationship.

Finally, the lack of commitment in marriage is largely because of the secular perspective we have of marriage. Many see marriage as a contractual agreement, rather than as a covenant. Contractual agreements are always temporary, and can easily be broken if the terms of the contract are not upheld. However, marriage is a covenant that we make, not only with each other, but with God. It is also a vow that is made before God and man, that says, for better or worse, richer or poorer, in sickness or in health, we will stay together until death. It is completely different from a contract. In fact, the Bible has this to say about vows, *"It is better not to make a vow than to make one and not fulfill it"* Ecclesiastes 5:5 (NIV).

It is imperative therefore, that you check to ensure that you are able to commit to your marriage vows before you say I do. Failing that, you will not be able to avoid divorce, even with good intentions. So, make the decision today that you will examine yourself, change the faulty preconceptions you have of marriage and learn the art of commitment before you say, I do. Then you can expect to have a long and lasting relationship.

CONCLUSION

Statistics confirm that marriages are failing at an alarming rate. The lack of commitment among couples, the poor decision in choosing the right mate and the purposeless living among husbands and wives, all point to the fact that we are not following God's biblical principles for marriage. Evidence also shows that failure to prepare for marriage has repeatedly yielded the same result — divorce. The unrealistic expectations and poor management skills that are carried into a marriage are all indicators, that not enough preparation was done beforehand.

Therefore, having a marriage that is divorce-proof and immensely successful does not happen by accident. Neither does finding the right mate occur by chance. These occurrences happen because men and women discovered God's truth concerning marriage and applied those principles to their lives. They happen because persons were bold enough to divorce themselves from the secular teachings regarding marriage and accept God's perspective.

To avoid being a victim of a failed marriage and to not be among the many unhappy couples who are enduring their marriages, rather than enjoying it, you must not only adopt God's biblical principles for marriage, but practically work them out in your life in preparation for a lasting union.

REFERENCES

[i] *Marriage & Divorce : APA*. (n.d.). Retrieved July 5, 2016, from APA Web site: http://www.apa.org/

[ii] *Divorces in England and Wales: 2013 : ONS*. (2015, Nov 23). Retrieved July 5, 2016, from ONS Web site: http://www.ons.gov.uk

[iii] *Divorce Statistics : divorcestatistics* . (n.d.). Retrieved July 5, 2016, from divorcestatistics Web site: http://www.divorcestatistics.org/

[iv] *New Marriage and Divorce Statistics Released : barna*. (2008, March 31). Retrieved July 12, 2016, from barna Web site: https://www.barna.org

[v] Caba, J. (2013, Nov 25). *Heavy Drinking Will Lead To Divorce, Unless Both Partners Are Equally Alcoholic : medicaldaily* . Retrieved Juky 27, 2016, from medicaldaily Web site: http://www.medicaldaily.com

[vi] *Everything You Need To Know About Divorce – Facts, Statistics, and Rates : wf-lawyers*. (n.d.). Retrieved July 27, 2016, from wf-lawyers Web site: http://www.wf-lawyers.com

[vii] *Survey: Certified Divorce Financial Analyst® (CDFA®) professionals Reveal the Leading Causes of Divorce : institutedfa*. (2016, July 12).

Retrieved from institutedfa Web site:
https://www.institutedfa.com

[viii] *Fighting with your spouse? It's probably about this :
cnbc*. (n.d.). Retrieved July 12, 2016, from cnbc
Web site: http://www.cnbc.com/

[ix] Fontinelle, A. (n.d.). *Budgeting Basics : investopedia*.
Retrieved July 12, 2016, from investopedia Web
site: http://www.investopedia.com

[x] *Poor Communication Is The #1 Reason Couples Split
Up: Survey : huffingtonpost*. (2013, Nov 20).
Retrieved August 7, 2016, from huffingtonpost
Web site: http://www.huffingtonpost.com

[xi] *New Expert Survey Reveals the Number One Reason
Couples Divorce : magazine.foxnews*. (2012,
October 15). Retrieved August 7, 2016, from
magazine.foxnews Web site:
http://magazine.foxnews.com/

[xii] *Everything You Need To Know About Divorce – Facts,
Statistics, and Rates : wf-lawyers*. (n.d.).
Retrieved August 12, 2016, from wf-lawyers:
http://www.wf-lawyers.com

[xiii] *Depression Increases Marital Dissatisfaction and
Divorce : usgs*. (n.d.). Retrieved August 12,
2016, from usgs: https://www2.usgs.gov

[xiv] *Sexual and reproductive health : who.* (2016, July 15). Retrieved from who Web site: http://www.who.int

[xv] *Infertility FAQs : cdc.* (2016, July 15). Retrieved from cdc Web site: http://www.cdc.gov/

[xvi] *How common is male infertility, and what are its causes? : nichd.* (n.d.). Retrieved August 30, 2016, from nichd: https://www.nichd.nih.gov

[xvii] *How common is male infertility, and what are its causes?: nichd.* (n.d.). Retrieved July 15, 2016, from nichd: https://www.nichd.nih.gov

[xviii] *Are Childless Couples Headed Toward Divorce? : huffingtonpost.* (n.d.). Retrieved August 30, 2016, from huffingtonpost: http://www.huffingtonpost.com

[xix] *When Guilty Father Syndrome Threatens Your Marriage : huffingtonpost.* (2011, Nov 17). Retrieved August 30, 2016, from huffingtonpost Web site: http://www.huffingtonpost.com/

Other Books on Amazon by this Author

1. Who Am I? Discovering Your Identity

2. From Faith to Faith

To Contact the Author

Email: dameyan2k@gmail.com